MW00900500

Fighter Pilot

Peggy J. Parks

KIDHAVEN PRESS
An imprint of Thomson Gale, a part of The Thomson Corporation

THOMSON
———— * ————™
GALE

Detroit • New York • San Francisco • San Diego
New Haven, Conn.• Waterville, Maine • London • Munich

The author wishes to thank Major Keith Roleff and Captain Jim Theisen for their helpful assistance with this book.

LIBRARY OF CONGRESS CATALOGING-IN-PUBLICATION DATA
Parks, Peggy J., 1951–
  Fighter pilot / By Peggy J. Parks.
    p. cm. — (Exploring careers)
  Includes bibliographical references and index.
  ISBN 0-7377-3079-X (hard cover : alk. paper) 1. Flight training—Juvenile litera-
ture. 2. Aeronautics, Military—Vocational guidance—Juvenile literature. 3. Fighter
pilots—Juvenile literature. 4. Airplanes—Piloting—Vocational guidance—Juvenile
literature. I. Title. II. Exploring careers (KidHaven Press)
  UG637.P37 2005
  358.4'383'0922—dc22
                                                                    2005018965

Printed in the United States of America

CONTENTS

Chapter 1
From Fighting Falcons
to Super Hornets   4

Chapter 2
What It Takes to Be a Fighter Pilot   12

Chapter 3
Fighter Pilots on the Job   20

Chapter 4
Meet a Fighter Pilot   29

Notes   39

Glossary   41

For Further Exploration   43

Index   45

Picture Credits   47

About the Author   48

From Fighting Falcons to Super Hornets

When pilots climb into the cockpit of a fighter jet, strap themselves in, take off and streak across the sky like lightning, they do it for one reason: to serve their country. Fighter pilots are elite military officers. The jets they fly are the most powerful, sophisticated, and expensive aircraft in the world. In the United States, they work for the Marine Corps, Navy, Air National Guard, and Air Force. They may be stationed in the United States or at military bases in other countries.

Flying War Missions

Many Air Force fighter pilots fly jets known as F-16 Fighting Falcons. These aircraft can reach speeds of

1,500 miles (2,400km) per hour. That is amazingly fast—about twice as fast as the speed of sound! Like all fighter pilots, those who fly F-16s can carry a number of advanced weapons on their missions. Guns and missiles allow them to shoot down enemy aircraft in a type of air-to-air combat called a **dogfight**. F-16 pilots also carry bombs that are known as **smart bombs.** Lasers or global positioning satellites guide the bombs so they hit only the exact target they seek. Journalist Tom Neven explains this level of precision: "If they want to put a bomb through the third window on the left, they literally can."[1]

Flying Daredevils

The Wild Weasels are F-16 fighter pilots who are known as the "daredevils of the skies" because the work they do is so dangerous. The Wild Weasels' job is to seek out enemy **antiaircraft artillery**. These missiles are like huge explosive darts that enemies shoot at aircraft from the ground. Many are guided by radar so they can pinpoint an aircraft with precision, and then chase it around the sky until they hit and destroy it.

Fighter jets are outfitted with tracking devices that let pilots know when the enemy has turned on radar. If the pilots detect radar, they use complicated maneuvering techniques and great speed to stay out of the missiles' way. The Wild Weasels, however, go hunting for radar, and in the process, they become flying targets.

Once the Weasel pilots detect that enemy radar has been turned on, the deadly race begins. Using their own powerful missiles, they try to destroy the ground radar systems and weapons before the enemy can fire. Then other allied fighter jets and bombers can move in for the attack. Air Force colonel Greg Ihde describes the typical attitude of the Wild Weasels: "It's not like we're crazy, but it takes someone with a lot of guts to want to waltz in and have a bad guy 'light you up.' You drive in and hope somebody wants to shoot at your airplane. Then we go to work."[2]

Protecting the United States

Fighter pilots like the Wild Weasels are based in war zones and fly regular combat missions. But there are also fighter pilots whose job is to protect airspace in the United States. One of them is Lieutenant Tim Lehmann, who flies an F-16 for the Air National Guard. In May 2005, Lehmann was involved in a situation that was potentially threatening for the nation's capital. His base received an alert that a small Cessna airplane was headed for the White House. The Cessna pilot had ignored warnings from air traffic controllers and entered a restricted air zone around Washington, D.C. Lehmann and another fighter pilot immediately jumped in their F-16s and took off.

The two fighter pilots reached the small plane and began circling it. Unable to reach the pilot on

The job of fighter pilots like these is to protect the United States both at home and abroad.

Some fighter pilots fly F-16 fighter jets like the ones pictured here.

the radio, Lehmann fired a warning signal with a flare. When the pilot did not respond, Lehmann continued circling the plane. He fired a second flare and then a third. Finally, when the Cessna was just three miles from the White House, the pilot changed course and started traveling away from the restricted zone.

Later, it was determined that the pilot had gotten confused and was not actually a threat. However, the two F-16 pilots had the authority to shoot the small plane down if necessary. In an interview with CNN, Lehmann emphasized his commitment to doing whatever it takes to protect U.S. airspace: "I'd like to assure your listeners that that airplane would not have penetrated—it would not have hit anything in D.C. And it would have been dropped from the sky before that would have happened."[3]

Takeoffs and Landings at Sea

When Lehmann and other F-16 pilots take off and land, they use ground landing strips. This is different from pilots who fly for the Navy and Marines. These pilots fly jets such as the F/A-18 Hornet and Super Hornet, and the F-14 Tomcat, which are designed to take off from and land on huge ships known as **aircraft carriers**. Pilots are able to take off from the ships because of **catapults** mounted on the deck. Catapults are like monstrous slingshots propelled by steam, and they are extremely powerful. They can launch a fighter jet off a ship and send it flying into the air—from 0 to 175 miles (282km) per hour—in only two seconds.

Some fighter pilots are specially trained to take off and land at sea on enormous ships known as aircraft carriers.

One of the most challenging jobs for a fighter pilot is landing a jet on an aircraft carrier. As large as the ship's deck is, pilots still must land in a space that is a fraction of the size of a ground landing strip. They can do this because the tails of the fighter jets are fitted with a long hook known as a **tailhook**. The pilots must snag their tailhook on one of four heavy-duty wire cables stretched across the deck. A Marine fighter pilot whose **call sign** (nickname) is Rooster describes what the experience is like: "It is extremely difficult to land at high speed on a platform that is moving up and down, and swaying from left to right, wet with water from ocean waves. When you land, the jet is racing toward the end of the ship and then suddenly the hook catches with such a jolt that you swear you're going to be thrown out."[4]

Pilots must anticipate the moment when they are about to touch down on the aircraft carrier's deck. The second they do, they start to race the jet's engines at full power. That way if they miss the cables, they can take off again and give the landing another try. "But by that time," adds Rooster, "you will be a little more tired and will have a little less gas, so you'd better make it work!"[5]

War Zones

Fighter pilots are officers with the Marines, Navy, Air Force, or Air National Guard. Some are stationed in war zones, while others are assigned to protect airspace in the United States. They fly powerful jets that are armed with sophisticated weapons. Yet no matter what branch of the military they work for, where they are based, or what type of jet they fly, their job is to protect and serve their country.

A crew prepares to catapult an F/A-18 jet off the flight deck of the USS *Kitty Hawk*.

CHAPTER 2

What It Takes to Be a Fighter Pilot

Fighter pilots in all branches of the military are well aware that their jobs are prestigious. Marine Corps major Keith Roleff offers a description of the typical fighter pilot: "Very self-confident, highly competitive, borderline arrogant, cocky, and brash personality."[6] Roleff and other high-ranking military officers stress that these qualities are essential for fighter pilots. They must be 100 percent sure of themselves at all times. When they are flying, they cannot afford to lose focus even for a split second. Theirs is a job with absolutely no room for error. They are aware that if they make mistakes, lives could be lost—including their own.

Officer candidates in training must undergo grueling physical conditioning.

Becoming an Officer

It takes a long time before pilots become qualified to fly fighter jets. The education and training they go through is tough, involved, and highly stressful. Their first step is to earn a bachelor's degree from college. After choosing their preferred branch of the military, they undergo extensive testing. If they qualify, they can enroll in officer training.

Those who join the Navy or Marines must attend officer candidate school (OCS) toward the end of their college program. Military instructors push the trainees hard to see how much physical and mental stress they can handle, as Rooster explains: "OCS is designed to tear you in half. They want to see how tough you are, and whether you fold under pressure. They're constantly testing you, seeing how far they can push before you finally break."

He adds, however, that there is a good reason why OCS is so tough: "It gives people a taste of what they can expect in combat situations. During wartime, officers must keep a level head no matter what happens. If they cannot handle the pressure in OCS, they will not be able to handle it when they are really at war."[7]

Advanced officer training is even tougher. Students participate in rigorous physical fitness routines and are tested often on their strength and endurance. They learn about the history and

Marines in combat training participate in exercises to learn skills they will need in actual combat.

mission of their particular branch of the military. They are taught how to march in formation, how to lead, and how to be part of a team.

Throughout their training, students are constantly reminded that their number one job is to prepare for war. They study combat tactics, principles of war, and war history. They learn about every type of weapon and how those weapons work. They are taught how to take weapons apart and put them back together, and they perfect their shooting skills at target ranges.

Learning to Fly

After officer training, students start learning how to be pilots. This begins with preflight training, where they learn everything there is to know about flying before leaving the ground. They attend classes to learn about aircraft systems, including engines and cockpit instruments. They study flight regulations, mission planning, and navigation. They put in twelve-hour days, and they have very little free time. Even when they are not in class, they are expected to be in their rooms studying.

After preflight training, aspiring pilots are finally ready to fly. They start out in **simulators**, which have mock cockpits used for practice. Students learn how to use all the aircraft's controls and instruments, including how to handle every possible emergency. After a few days on the ground, they begin flying in a trainer aircraft with an instructor.

They practice takeoffs and landings over and over again, and learn to fly in close formation with other planes. They are also trained in instrument flying, which is when a pilot flies a plane by relying solely on instruments for guidance, rather than sight. Throughout the training, students are graded on their skills and knowledge. At the end, the scores are tallied and the trainees are rated. Only a select few in the top of the class can advance to the next level—learning to fly fighter jets.

Preparing for War

Fighter pilot training consists of classroom instruction, simulator training, and actual flying in a fighter jet. Students must memorize every inch of the aircraft and become completely familiar with all the controls and instruments. Since the job of a fighter pilot is to be ready for war, the training focuses on combat. Captain Mike Balfany of the Air National Guard explains why this is essential: "You want to train the way you fight. If you're ever going to fly and be effective in combat, you have to have realistic training. Everything we do is driven by the fact that someday we might have to engage in combat."[8]

To practice dogfighting skills, pilots participate in mock battles with planes that are painted to look like enemy aircraft. They practice **aerobatics**, such as rolls, spins, dives, and fancy turns—all of which are intended to outsmart enemy aircraft by maneuvering around it. They also practice dropping real

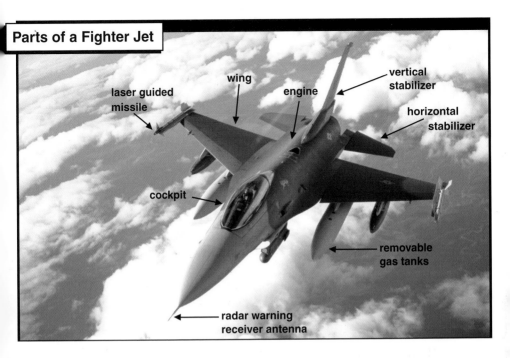

Parts of a Fighter Jet

wing

laser guided missile

engine

vertical stabilizer

horizontal stabilizer

cockpit

removable gas tanks

radar warning receiver antenna

bombs in specially designated ranges where giant targets are painted on the ground. Rooster says when people miss their targets, they are strongly reprimanded by instructors. "No matter how good of a pilot you are, if you can't kill an enemy to protect your fellow soldiers, what good are you? Any time you can't perform it's a strike against you—enough strikes and you're thrown out of flight school."[9]

By far, the most challenging part of fighter pilot training is learning to land a jet. This is especially nerve-racking for those in the Navy or Marines because their landing platform is a wobbling, rocking aircraft carrier. Long before they actually land on a ship, they practice hundreds of times on landing strips that are painted to simulate a ship's deck.

A fighter pilot engages in a practice dogfight.

Still, when the time arrives to land the plane for the first time, it is a frightening experience, as Rooster explains: "When the instructor called my name out on the radio, I was more scared than I've ever been in my life. You rely totally on instincts because you're too freaked out to think. That's where all the training and practice comes in. Even though your brain shrinks down to about the size of a pea, your instincts kick in and carry you through."[10] Rooster's first landing was successful. But he says it took him a while before he was able to stop shaking.

Achieving a Dream

Throughout fighter pilot school, students are repeatedly tested on their skills. At the end of the training, the instructors tally everyone's score. Assignments are made based on which aircraft pilots want to fly, and whether or not their qualifications match up with their request. Only those pilots who have proven themselves to be superior in all categories are granted their first choice. Once they know which aircraft they will fly, the fighter pilots attend the last phase of their training. This is where they master the techniques of their own fighter jet. When they graduate, they are awarded their prestigious fighter pilot wings.

Fighter pilots have worked extremely hard to get where they are. They have invested many years in education and training and have endured tough physical conditioning. Along the way, they have proven they are the best of the best; their reward is flying the aircraft of their dreams.

CHAPTER 3

Fighter Pilots on the Job

Fighter pilots' jobs are far from dull. They never know quite what to expect from one day to the next. They may be assigned to a war zone where they fly combat missions, or they could be stationed in the United States where they spend their time training for war. Their jobs are dangerous, and their stress level is often high. They know they are going to face enemies, and when they do, they must be willing to take lives. Commanding Officer Jeff Penfield, a fighter pilot who flies a Super Hornet, explains this: "My job is to hit whatever target I've been assigned to hit. I don't think about it as human life. I aim at hard things, and if there are people around, I don't think about it."[11]

Combat pilots use laser-guided missiles, like the one shown here, against enemy targets.

Bombing Missions

In wartime, fighter pilots are assigned to fly missions by their commanding officers. In many cases they take off and head for a combat zone without knowing what their mission will be. This was the case when Rooster was stationed in Afghanistan in 2001. In the middle of the night, he took off from an aircraft carrier in the Arabian Sea. When he was in the air, he was told about a valley where there was an enemy headquarters called an outpost. Whenever ground troops tried to get through the valley, they were driven back by machine gun fire. Rooster's assignment was to find and destroy the outpost.

Guided by a central command source known as CentCom, Rooster located his target. From his position 3 miles (4.8km) above the ground, he dropped a powerful bomb that was guided by a global positioning system. The bomb hit the outpost and demolished it. Rooster describes the aftermath: "I have never in my life seen such a huge fireball—it must have been about a mile long. I was a long way up but I could see that explosion and I knew I had hit a fuel storage facility or munitions bunker or something. Whatever was in that valley before wasn't there anymore when I got done with it."[12]

On the second part of the mission, Rooster was ordered to proceed north from the valley. An armored enemy vehicle similar to a tank was believed

Dust and smoke rise from the ground after American pilots drop bombs on a village in Afghanistan in 2001.

This photograph shows bombs falling from an F-16 Fighting Falcon.

to be located there. It was mounted with four huge rapid-firing antiaircraft guns. CentCom directed Rooster to search for the vehicle and destroy it. The first thing he saw was a line of enemy troops in a trench. He fired at them but missed, so he was preparing to strike again using laser-guided bombs. Just then he saw the armored vehicle come around a hill. He redirected his laser instrument and hit the vehicle with a bomb. Rooster says the explosion was so violent that he saw a massive chunk of the vehicle go flying up a mountain in the opposite direction.

A Life-or-Death Situation

On some bombing missions, fighter pilots run into serious trouble. This happened to Captain Christina Hopper, a fighter pilot with the Air Force. She was flying an F-16 Fighting Falcon during the Iraq war on a night when the weather was extremely nasty. Driving rain was pelting her aircraft, and she was nearly blinded by blowing sand. At the same time, enemies on the ground were firing at her with surface-to-air missiles. Suddenly lightning struck Hopper's jet and destroyed its threat warning system—which meant she could not tell if she was being targeted by enemy radar. It was a deadly situation, but she refused to turn back. She completed her mission and bombed the enemy target. For her courage and brave actions, Hopper earned an Air Medal, one of the military's highest honors.

Seek and Destroy

Besides bombing missions, fighter pilots also participate in **reconnaissance**. On these missions, pilots fly through enemy territory for the purpose of seeking information. They use sophisticated radar equipment and cameras to survey the terrain below and record enemy activities. The photos can be immediately transmitted to commanders on the ground.

In armed reconnaissance missions, fighter pilots do more than just survey. They are given a supply of air-to-air missiles, air-to-ground missiles, and bombs. Then they fly out and start scouting a particular area. Rooster calls these "hunting trips" and says they are his favorite type of assignment: "We just ride around for hours and talk to Cent-Com on the radio. Throughout the trip, they say, 'Tell us what you see down there on the ground and we'll tell you whether it's the bad guys or not.' If it is, we fire on them with our weapons and then take off to hunt for more bad guys."[13]

Fighter pilots who fly reconnaissance missions take photographs like this one to locate enemy targets.

The F-16 Fighting Falcon is so advanced that it is able to fly straight up.

War Games

Rooster says that even when fighter pilots are back in the United States, they constantly train and practice as if they were at war. Some days they attend classes to learn about the enemy.

Military personnel who have just returned from combat zones share recent information about enemy aircraft, weapons, and war tactics. This information is used to plan future missions.

In addition to classroom training, fighter pilots spend a lot of time flying and practicing with their aircraft's weapons. They participate in "war games," or mock battles. One area where this takes place is a military base known as Twentynine Palms. It is an enormous complex located on 90 square miles (233 sq km) in the California desert. Pilots practice their air-to-ground weapons skills by dropping bombs on ground targets. On some days, they do not fly. Instead, they pretend they have been stranded in enemy territory. During these exercises, the pilots spend two or three days camping in the desert to practice their land survival tactics.

Combat Practice

Fighter pilots also perfect their dogfighting skills at Twentynine Palms. This type of battle is no longer common in war zones because enemies favor antiaircraft missiles over air-to-air combat. However, pilots must be prepared to fight in the air if necessary. The dogfighting exercises are very realistic. First, fighter pilots must be absolutely sure they are facing a person who is playing the role of enemy. They do this by using radar and also by using their superior aerobatic skills.

They maneuver their jets by flipping, rolling, spinning, and turning, in order to get close to the other aircraft. If they determine that it is the pretend enemy, they shoot with fake missiles. Rooster says this is much like two dogs chasing each other so they can bite off each other's tails—but this chase is happening at 400 miles (644km) per hour. "During a dogfight," he says, "my goal is to out-maneuver the bad guy and get myself in a position where he can't get away. So no matter what he does, I'll be able to fire on him and he can't shoot back at me. When this happens in real life, it's a live-or-die situation so fighter pilots must have the mentality of always being able to win."[14]

At the end of these combat practice sessions, fighter pilots land their aircraft and then have a meeting. Throughout the mock battles, cameras have tracked the pilots' performance. They can watch all the action replayed on a computer monitor. Then they discuss what they did right and what they did wrong, and how they can perform better next time.

Fighter pilots have jobs that are exciting, challenging, and dangerous. They may be assigned to combat zones where they bomb enemy targets, or fly reconnaissance missions to survey enemy territory. When they are not at war, their job is to practice and prepare for war. From one day to the next, their jobs may be very different. What they all share is the commitment to use their training, experience, and skills to serve their country.

CHAPTER 4

Meet a Fighter Pilot

A fighter pilot who goes by the call sign of Barney has a job that many people only dream about. Barney flies an F/A-18 Hornet for the U.S. Marine Corps. He says unlike most people in his career, he did not grow up dreaming of being a fighter pilot. He actually thought he would be a truck driver someday. However, when he heard about the Marines' college reimbursement program, he decided to enlist. At that point he still did not plan to make a career out of the military.

When Barney became aware of the opportunities in military aviation, he decided to apply for flight school. He was accepted and almost immediately found that he had a talent for flying. He excelled at his studies and won a spot in the Marines' fighter pilot training program. The first

A fighter pilot stands on the runway beside his F/A-18 Hornet.

time he got behind the controls of a fighter jet, there was no turning back. "I was hooked from the start," he says. "What I do is exciting and fun and I feel very, very fortunate to be a fighter pilot. How many people have an opportunity to fly an incredible aircraft like the Hornet? But beyond that, I also consider it an honor and a privilege to do this job." When asked if fighter pilots are as fearless as they are portrayed in the movies, Barney is quick with an answer: "Yes we are, and yes I am. Of course we're aware that what we do is dangerous, but we have a job to do and we don't focus on the danger. And we all think we're the best there is—every fighter pilot feels that way. We're pretty sure of ourselves."[15]

Memorable Mission

Barney says the most rewarding time for a fighter pilot is when a mission goes exactly as planned. He shares an example of one such time:

> I was the commander during an Operation Iraqi Freedom mission in 2002. Our orders were to fly into Baghdad and bomb an enemy antiaircraft missile zone known as a SuperMEZ. No one had ever flown that far south in Iraq before, and heading straight for an area with all those missiles ready to blow us out of the air was pretty dangerous stuff.

We launched off the carrier USS *Truman* and flew toward Baghdad, which was a trip of about 700 miles [1,100km]. When we reached the zone, we had our electronic jammers on so the enemy's radar couldn't track us and we started dropping our bombs. Then I lost radio contact with my AIC [air intercept controller], so I couldn't let him know that I was running low on fuel. By the time we finished the mission and started heading back north, I literally had seconds left before my fuel would be gone—and Baghdad is not a place where a U.S. fighter jet wants to land and beg for gas! Just then I got the AIC back on the radio and an air tanker came to put fuel in my aircraft. I remember saying to the pilot, "Man, you don't get any closer than that!" It was a two-hour flight back to the ship and by the time I landed, I was hungry, thirsty, and exhausted. But the mission went flawlessly—we destroyed the enemy's Super-MEZ and knowing that was an exhilarating feeling. Later I was awarded an Individual Action Air Medal for heroic action, which was quite an honor.

Frustrating Experience
Barney recalls another mission in Iraq that did not go so well:

An Air Force tanker refuels a fighter jet in midflight.

It was during some nasty thunderstorms and the clouds were so thick that we couldn't get out of them no matter how high we went. We flew for more than two hours through that horrid weather and were literally bounced all over the sky the whole time. As much as I love flying, it is not enjoyable to fly in those conditions—

An F/A-18 Hornet lands on a wet runway. Pilots must be especially careful when landing in wet conditions.

my knuckles were white from gripping the controls so tightly. We knew there were U.S. troops on the ground who needed our support and we wanted to help them but we couldn't. The weather prevented us from doing anything, and we had to turn around and go back. We spent all that time and effort, putting ourselves at risk and not even being able to do one thing to help the guys who needed us. By the time I landed on that ship I was both angry and frustrated. . . . That's the kind of mission you don't feel good about.

A Close Call

Another of Barney's encounters with bad weather was especially frightening. Early in his military career he was stationed in Japan. One night he was practicing his instrument flying. He was taking off from, and landing on, a runway, rather than an aircraft carrier. He could see that thunderstorms had started to roll in and were getting closer, so he was about to make his final landing. He explains what happened next:

I radioed the guy in the control tower to ask whether there was standing water on the runway. Hornets have very little tread on the tires and if you try to land in slick conditions, the jet can skid out of control.

He told me the runway was wet but there was no standing water, so I went in for the landing—and soon found out he was wrong. I was about halfway down the runway, going probably 175 miles [280km] per hour, and the aircraft started skidding and almost went sideways. At that point, you don't think, you just react. I kicked the rudder and pushed all the power I had so I could climb back up again. Then I started screaming at the control tower guy, asking him what the heck he was thinking! I was low on fuel and I had to land but the runway wasn't safe, so he told me to do an arrested landing. That's where you land on a runway that's equipped with the same hook and cable system they have on aircraft carriers. I put my hook down, grabbed the wire, and came to a stop. I don't think I've ever been so relieved to be back on the ground.

Barney explains why that type of situation can be so dangerous: "Another fighter pilot I knew ran into the same problem and his jet ran off the runway. The tip of the wing caught on the ground and it spun the jet around, causing it to flip over and cartwheel. It was tragic because the pilot was killed in the accident."

A fighter pilot walks away from his jet after landing on the USS *Kitty Hawk*.

Parting Words

When asked if he would recommend his career to young people, Barney says he absolutely would. "I thank God I've had the opportunity to do this and I'm convinced it's the best job in the world. It's thrilling and challenging, as well as immensely satisfying." However, he also has some strong words of advice for aspiring fighter pilots:

> Stay in school, go to college, don't do drugs, and keep yourself physically fit. People see fighter pilots and think it's a glamorous job, but what they don't realize is that flying is only part of it. We're people who are very dedicated and driven. We work hard, we stay out of trouble, and we play by the rules. If you're not willing to do that, you're not welcome in our club. And if you are, well . . . maybe someday I'll meet you up in the wild blue.

NOTES

Chapter 1:
From Fighting Falcons
to Super Hornets

1. Tom Neven, "Stealth Force," *Breakaway*, August 2002, p. 16.

2. Quoted in Jason Tudor, "Spangdahlem Wild Weasels Gouge Enemy Eyes," *Airman*, July 2002. www.af.mil/news/airman/0702/sead.html.

3. Quoted in Kyra Phillips, "F-16 Pilot: Intercept 'a Difficult Period,'" CNN.com, *CNN Access*, May 12, 2005. www.cnn.com/2005/US/05/12/cnna.lehmann.

4. Rooster (Marine fighter pilot), interview with author, June 10, 2005.

5. Rooster, interview with author.

Chapter 2:
What It Takes
to Be a Fighter Pilot

6. Major Keith Roleff, interview with author, May 27, 2005.

7. Rooster, interview with author.

8. Quoted in "Today's Air National Guard: Why and How We Train," Defense Environmental Network & Information Exchange Public News. www.denix.osd.mil/denix/public/news/AF/A NG/train/ang.html.

9. Rooster, interview with author.

10. Rooster, interview with author.

Chapter 3:
Fighter Pilots on the Job

11. Quoted in Lyndsey Layton, "Causing Death and Destruction, but Never Seeing It," *Washington Post*, April 3, 2003, p. A31.

12. Rooster, interview with author.

13. Rooster, interview with author.

14. Rooster, interview with author.

Chapter 4:
Meet a Fighter Pilot

15. All quotes in Chapter 4, Marine fighter pilot Barney, interview with author, June 26, 2005.

GLOSSARY

aerobatics: Fancy stunts, such as rolls, dives, and spins, that fighter pilots use to outmaneuver the enemy during dogfights.

aircraft carriers: Enormous ships designed to launch fighter jets.

antiaircraft artillery: Powerful guns and missiles that are used to destroy aircraft.

catapults: Steam-powered mechanisms on aircraft carriers that launch fighter jets off the deck and into the air.

call sign: A nickname used to identify fighter pilots.

dogfight: Aerial combat between two fighter planes.

reconnaissance: A mission designed to survey enemy activities.

simulators: Devices or systems that help train fighter pilots in the operation of an aircraft.

smart bombs: Bombs that can be precisely directed toward an enemy target.

tailhook: The hook on a fighter jet that allows the jet to stop very suddenly when it snags a cable.

FOR FURTHER EXPLORATION

Books
Allison Stark Draper, *Fighter Pilots: Life at Mach Speed*. New York: Rosen, 2001. Describes the training fighter pilots go through, as well as the aircraft they fly and the weapons they use.

Robert C. Kennedy, *Life as an Air Force Fighter Pilot*. New York: Children's Press, a Division of Grolier, 2000. An in-depth look at the fighter pilot's job, including a very good description of training and interesting information about the history of aviation warfare.

Periodicals
Kathryn R. Hoffman, "A Courageous Crew: Life Aboard an Aircraft Carrier Is Always Action-Packed," *Time for Kids World Report Edition*, November 16, 2001.

Tom Neven, "Stealth Force," *Breakaway*, August 2002.

Web Sites

How Stuff Works—Science Channel
(http://science.howstuffworks.com). An information-packed site that covers the F/A-18 Hornet, smart bombs, ejection seats, and many other topics related to the job of fighter pilots.

PBS Battle of the X-Planes
(www.pbs.org/wgbh/nova/xplanes). This site has interviews with fighter pilots and interesting facts about their jobs, including details about the special G-suits pilots must wear whenever they fly.

U.S. Navy Blue Angels
(www.blueangels.navy.mil). An interesting site about the world-famous team of fighter jets that includes photos, historical information, and a list of answers to frequently asked questions about the Blue Angels.

INDEX

aerobatics, 16, 27–28
Afghanistan, 21–23
aircraft carriers, 9–10, 17–18
Air Force, 10
Air National Guard, 6, 8, 10
air-to-air combat, 5, 16–17, 27–28
antiaircraft artillery, 5
armed reconnaissance missions, 24–26
arrested landings, 36
assignments, 19

Balfany, Mike, 16
Barney
advice to aspiring pilots from, 38
background of, 29, 31
on landing in bad weather, 35–36
on missions in Iraq, 31–33, 35

catapults, 9
characteristics, 6, 12, 31

combat training, 16

"daredevils of the skies," 5–6
dogfights, 5, 16–17, 27–28

education, 13

F-14 Tomcats, 9
F-16 Fighting Falcons, 4–6, 8, 24
F/A-18 Hornets, 9, 35–36

global positioning systems, 5, 22
ground landing strips, 9

Hopper, Christina, 24

Ihde, Greg, 6
Iraq, 24, 31–33, 35

landings, 10, 17–18, 35–36
lasers, 5
Lehman, Tim, 6, 8

45

Marines, 9–10, 13, 17–18

Navy, 9–10, 13, 17–18
Neven, Tom, 5

officer candidate school
  (OCS), 13–14
officer training, 13–15
Operation Iraqi Freedom,
  31–33, 35

Penfield, Jeff, 20
physical fitness, 13–14
preflight training, 15

radar, 5–6, 24
reconnaissance, 24–26
Roleff, Keith, 12
Rooster
  in Afghanistan, 21–23
  on armed reconnaissance
    missions, 25
  on dogfights, 28
  on landings, 10, 18
  on officer candidate school,
    13–14
  on training and practice,
    17, 26

simulators, 15

smart bombs, 5
speeds
  of catapult launches, 9
  during dogfights, 28
  of F-16 Fighting Falcons,
    4–5
Super Hornets, 9
survival tactics, 27

tailhooks, 10
takeoffs, 9
threat warning systems, 24
training
  to become officers, 13–15
  for flight, 15–19
  ongoing, 26–28
Twentynine Palms, 27

United States airspace, 6, 8
USS Truman, 32

war games, 27–28
war missions, 4–6
  in Afghanistan, 21–23
  in Iraq, 24, 31–33, 35
  reconnaissance, 24–26
weather problems, 24, 33,
  35–36
Wild Weasels, 5–6

PICTURE CREDITS

ABOUT THE AUTHOR

Peggy J. Parks holds a bachelor of science degree from Aquinas College in Grand Rapids, Michigan, where she graduated magna cum laude. She has written more than 40 titles for Thomson Gale's KidHaven Press, Blackbirch Press, and Lucent Books imprints. Parks lives in Muskegon, Michigan, a town she says inspires her writing because of its location on the shores of Lake Michigan.